Fourth Position Preparatory Studies

for the cello

by Cassia Harvey

CHP260

©2014 by C. Harvey Publications All Rights Reserved.

www.charveypublications.com - print books
www.learnstrings.com - PDF downloadable books
www.harveystringarrangements.com - chamber music

A String

First Position

Fourth Position

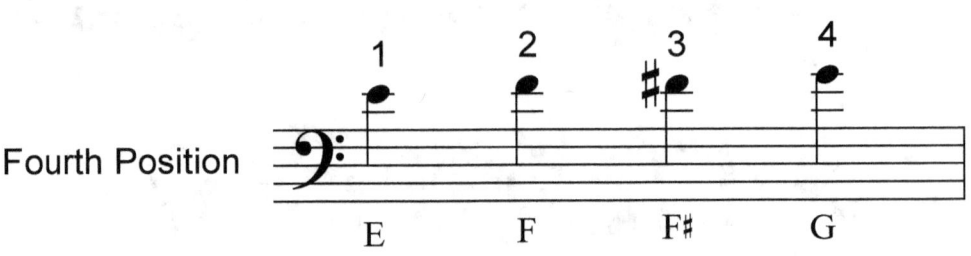

Fourth Position Preparatory Studies for Cello

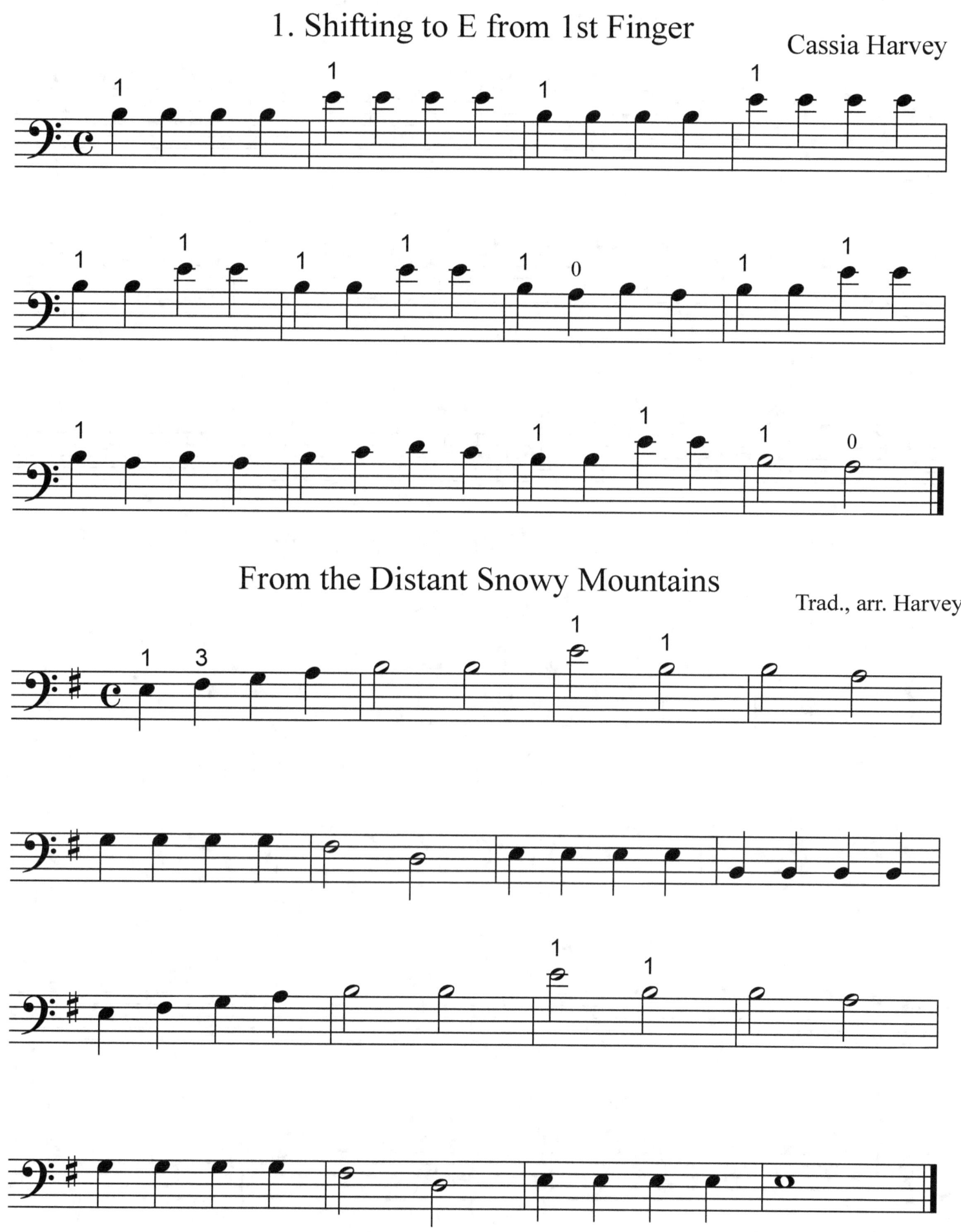

1. Shifting to E from 1st Finger — Cassia Harvey

From the Distant Snowy Mountains — Trad., arr. Harvey

©2014 C. Harvey Publications All Rights Reserved.

Fourth Position Preparatory Studies for Cello

2. Shifting to E in Rhythm

I Heard the Wild Geese Flying

Halvorsen, arr. Harvey

©2014 C. Harvey Publications All Rights Reserved.

Fourth Position Preparatory Studies for Cello

3. Shifting to E from 1st Finger

When Night is Falling

Targett, arr. Harvey

©2014 C. Harvey Publications All Rights Reserved.

4. Shifting to E from 2nd Finger

Big Bells Ringing

Trad., arr. Harvey

Fourth Position Preparatory Studies for Cello

5. Shifting to E in Rhythm

Sunrise

Harvey

©2014 C. Harvey Publications All Rights Reserved.

6. Shifting Back from E to 2nd Finger

The Tailor and the Mouse

Trad., arr. Harvey

Fourth Position Preparatory Studies for Cello

7. Shifting to E from 3rd Finger

Scaling the Peaks

Harvey

©2014 C. Harvey Publications All Rights Reserved.

8. Shortnin' Bread

Trad., arr. Harvey

White Dove

Trad., arr. Harvey

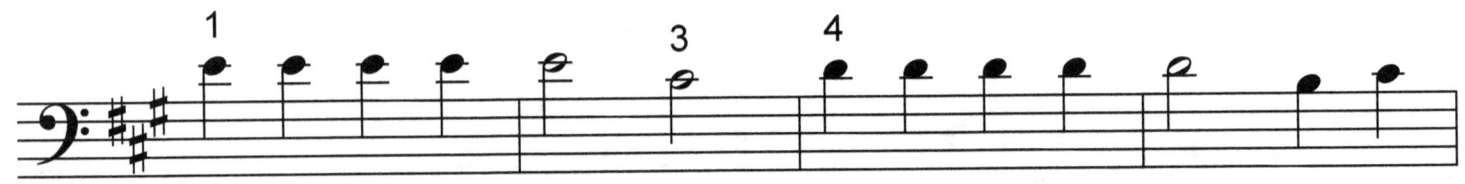

©2014 C. Harvey Publications All Rights Reserved.

Fourth Position Preparatory Studies for Cello

9. Shifting to E from 4th Finger

Bartolillo
Trad., arr. Harvey

©2014 C. Harvey Publications All Rights Reserved.

10. Nous n'irons plus au bois

Trad., arr. Harvey

Daffodils

Brockwell, arr. Harvey

Fourth Position Preparatory Studies for Cello

11. Shifting to E

Ah! mon beau Chateau

Trad., arr. Harvey

©2014 C. Harvey Publications All Rights Reserved.

12. Shifting to E from All Fingers

Oh, Susannah
Foster, arr. Harvey

Fourth Position Preparatory Studies for Cello 13

13. Shifting to 2nd Finger F

Pulsars
Harvey

©2014 C. Harvey Publications All Rights Reserved.

Fourth Position Preparatory Studies for Cello

15. More Shifting to F

Tadpoles

Forde, arr. Harvey

©2014 C. Harvey Publications All Rights Reserved.

16. Shifting to F from 3rd Finger

Quasars

Harvey

Fourth Position Preparatory Studies for Cello

17. Shifting to F from All Fingers

Promenade
Harvey

Fourth Position Preparatory Studies for Cello

18. Shifting to F from 4th Finger

The Pier
Harvey

©2014 C. Harvey Publications All Rights Reserved.

Fourth Position Preparatory Studies for Cello

19. Shifting to F#

Boutique Fantasque
Trad., arr. Harvey

©2014 C. Harvey Publications All Rights Reserved.

20. Shifting to F#

The Garnock Water
Ramsay, arr. Harvey

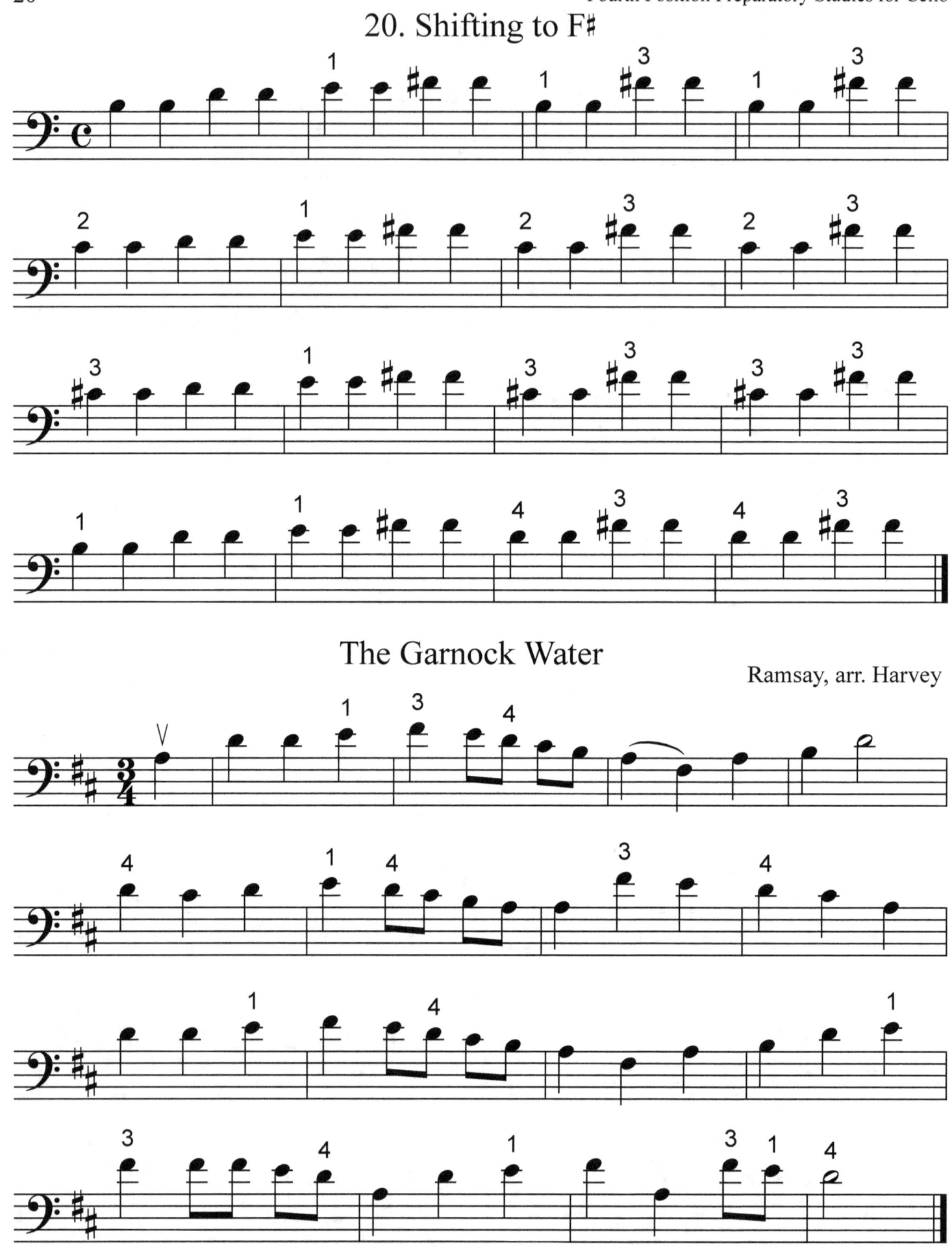

Fourth Position Preparatory Studies for Cello

21. Shifting to F#

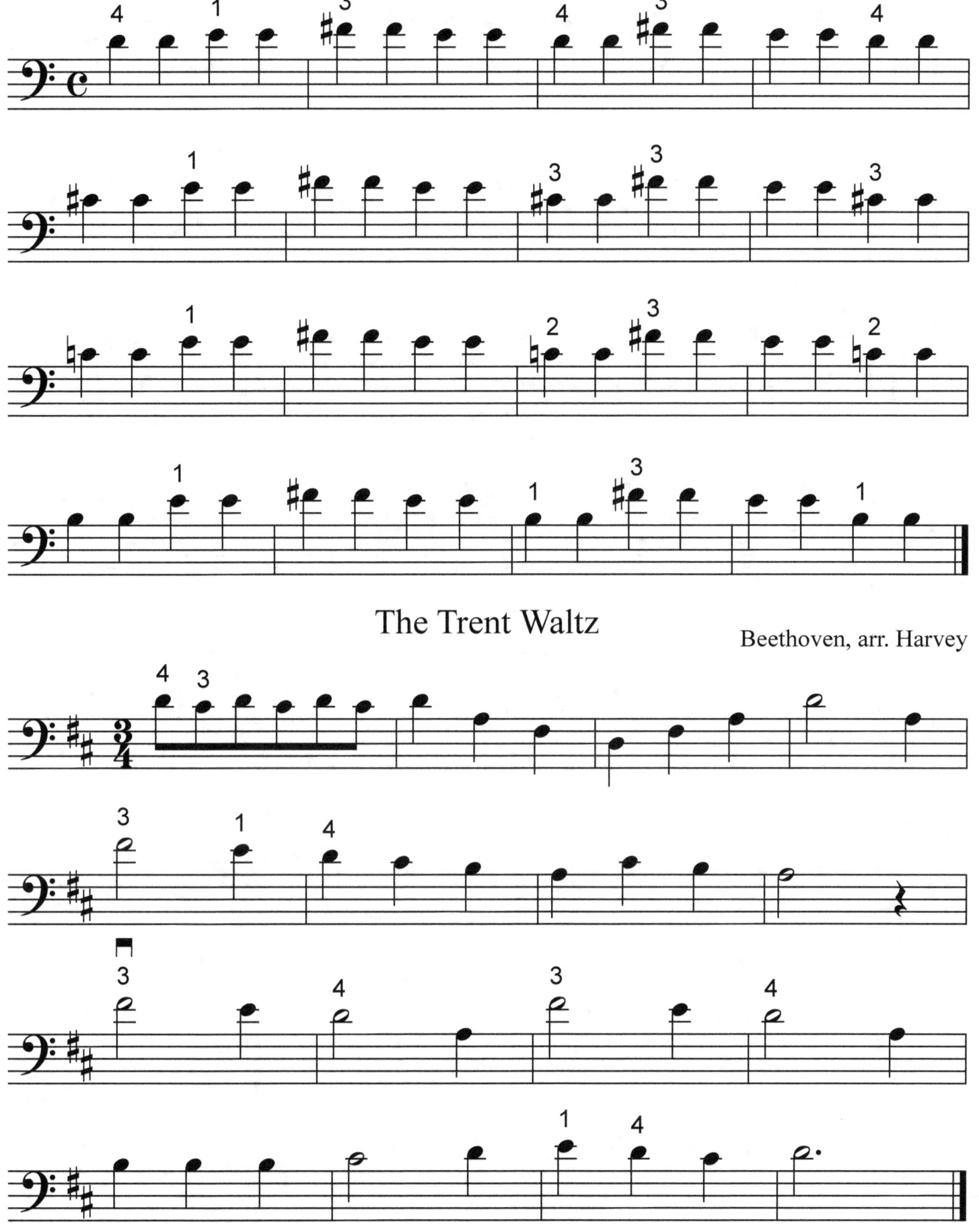

The Trent Waltz

Beethoven, arr. Harvey

©2014 C. Harvey Publications All Rights Reserved.

Fourth Position Preparatory Studies for Cello

23. Shifting to F# in Rhythm

The Grass Rustles

Trad., Harvey

©2014 C. Harvey Publications All Rights Reserved.

24. F# and F♮

The White Fish Played
Trad., arr. Harvey

Fourth Position Preparatory Studies for Cello

25. F# Review

Ukrainian Folk Song

Trad., arr. Harvey

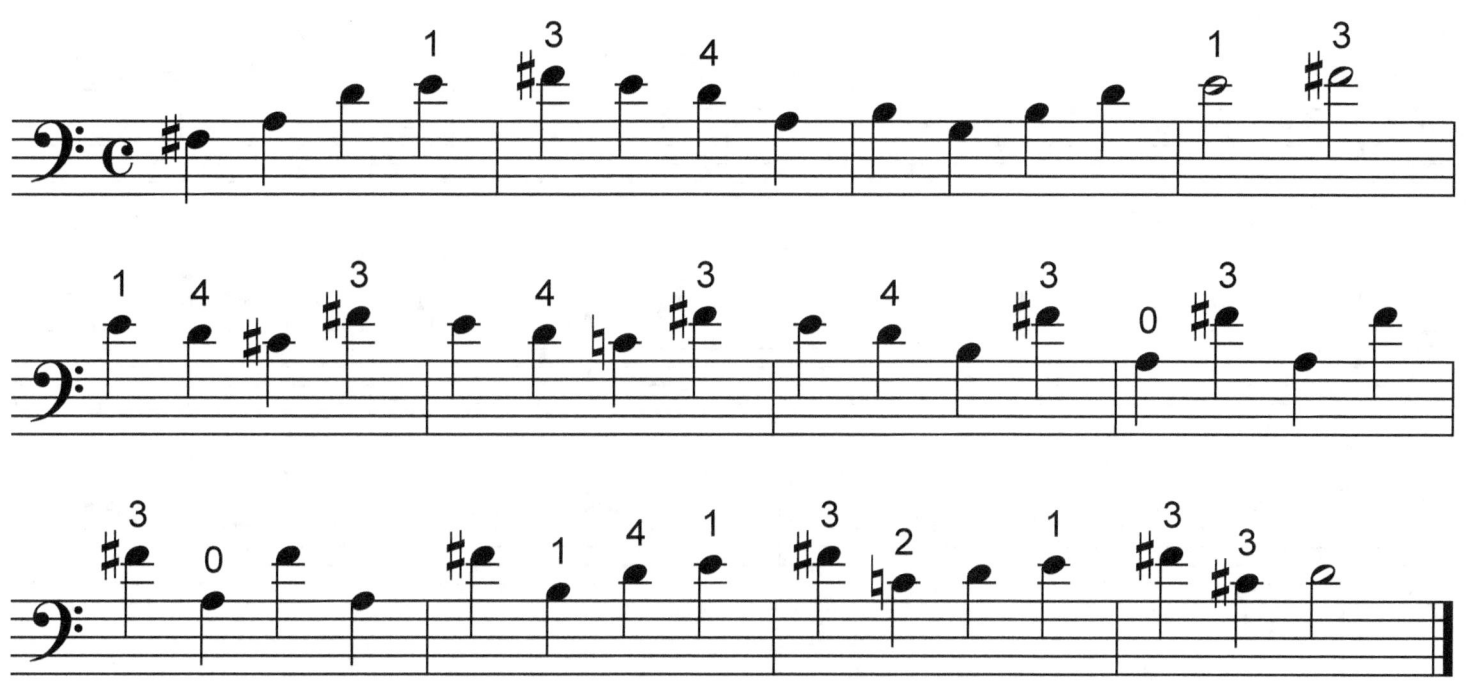

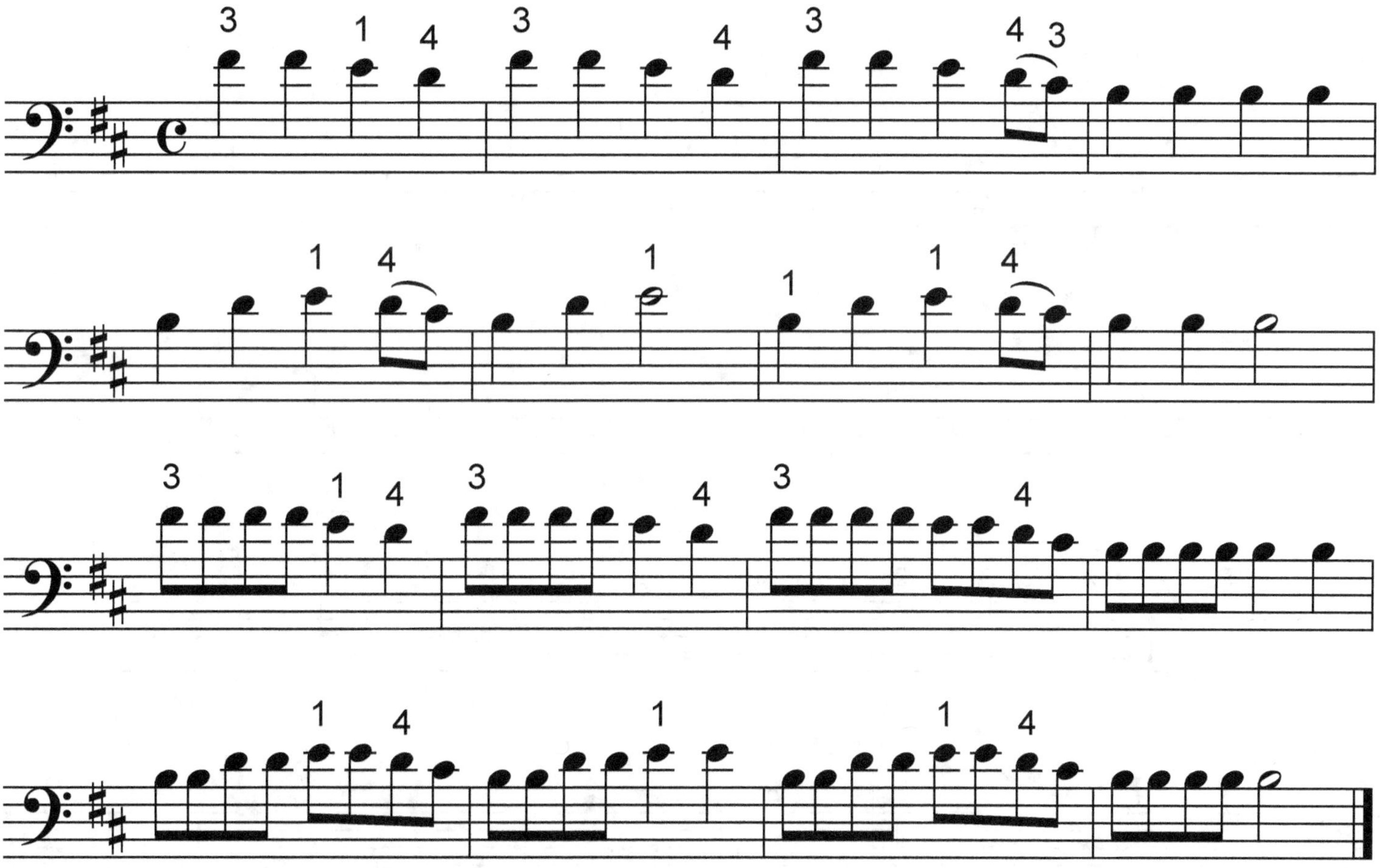

©2014 C. Harvey Publications All Rights Reserved.

26. Shifting to G

Aria
Bast, arr. Harvey

Fourth Position Preparatory Studies for Cello

27. Playing 4th Finger G

Oh, in Petrivochka the Night is Too Short

Trad., arr. Harvey

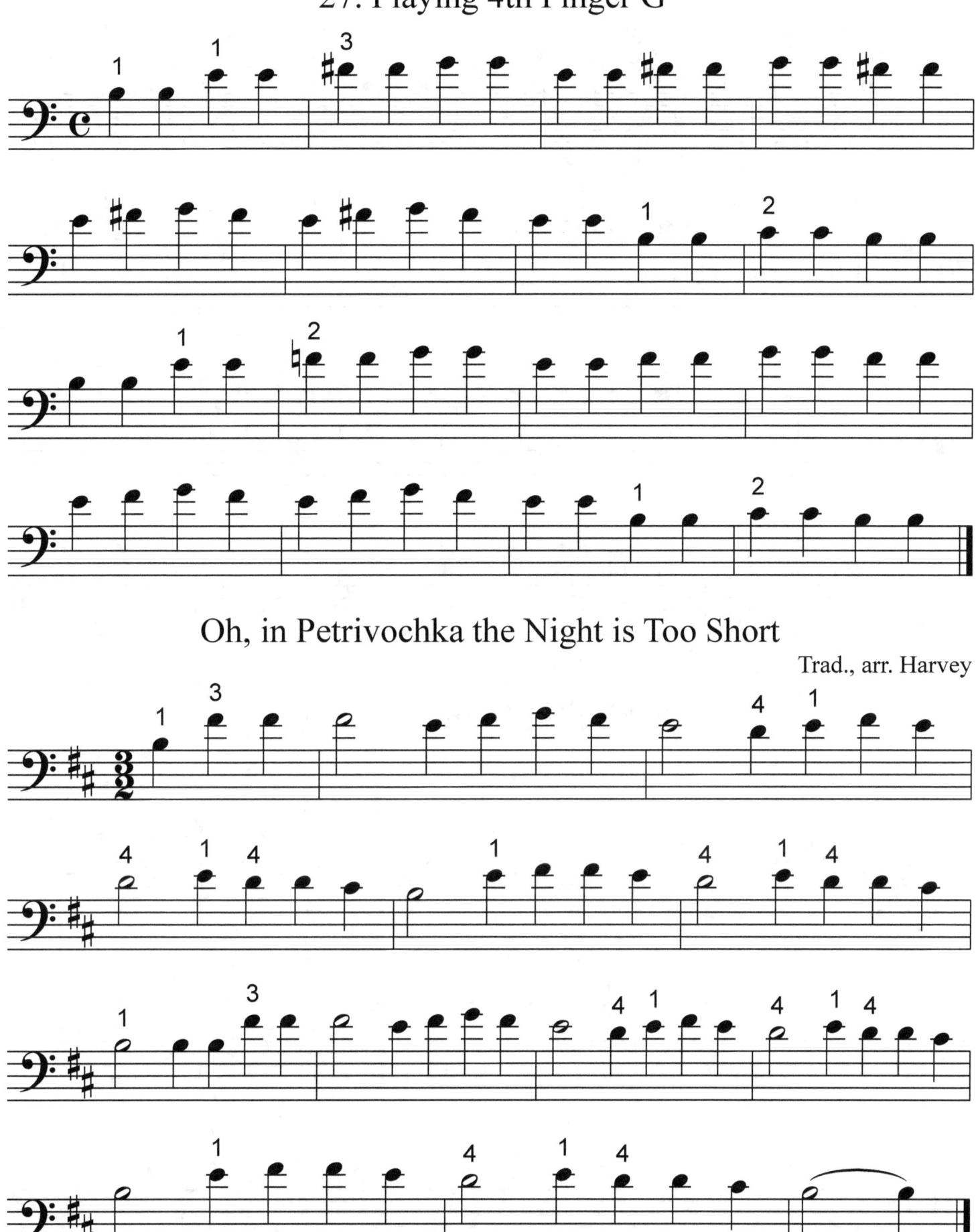

Fourth Position Preparatory Studies for Cello

28. Shifting to G

Oh Kumko, Borrow Barrels

Trad., arr. Harvey

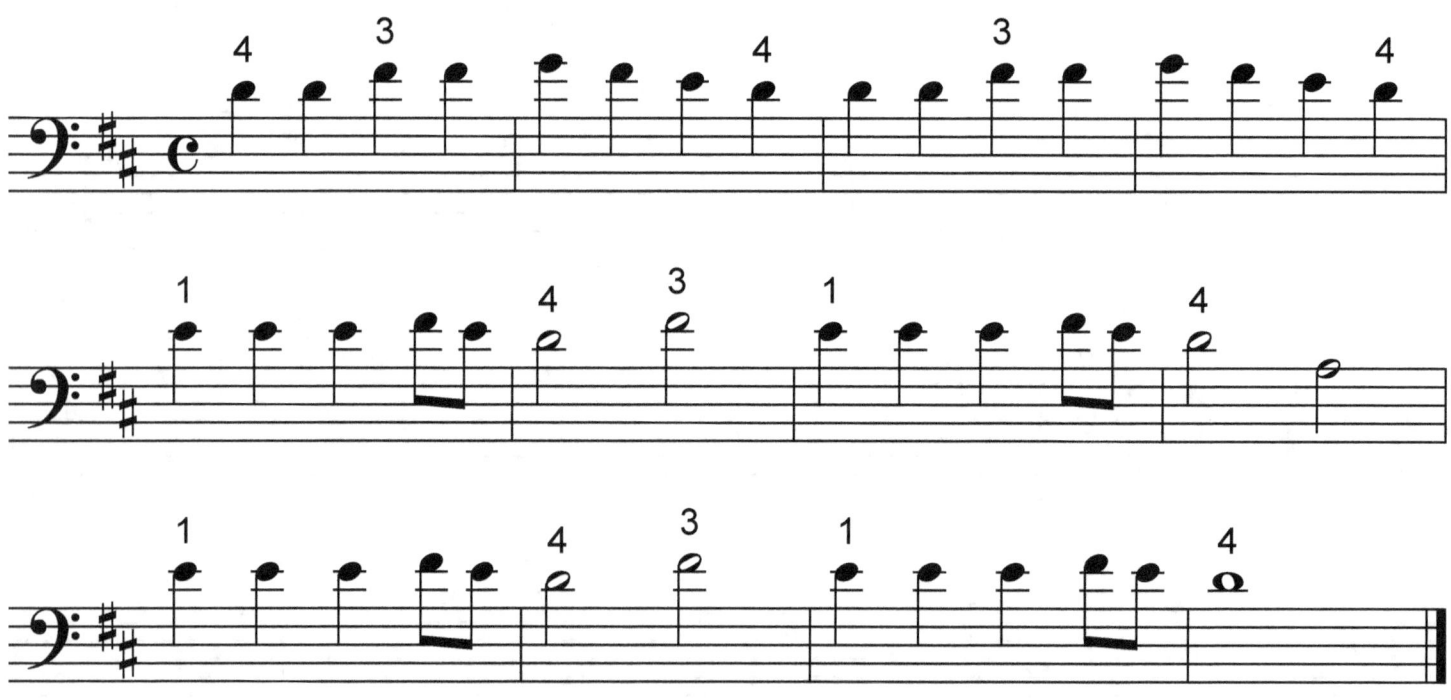

©2014 C. Harvey Publications All Rights Reserved.

Fourth Position Preparatory Studies for Cello

29. Shifting to F# and G

The Merry Allemande

Bast, arr. Harvey

Fourth Position Preparatory Studies for Cello

30. Using all Four Fingers

Danse Bohemienne
Von Weber, arr. Harvey

©2014 C. Harvey Publications All Rights Reserved.

Fourth Position Preparatory Studies for Cello

31. Using 2nd and 4th Fingers

Valse from 'Jordacki'

Von Weber, arr. Harvey

©2014 C. Harvey Publications All Rights Reserved.

Fourth Position Preparatory Studies for Cello

32. Finger Exercise

Rigaudon
Bast, arr. Harvey

©2014 C. Harvey Publications All Rights Reserved.

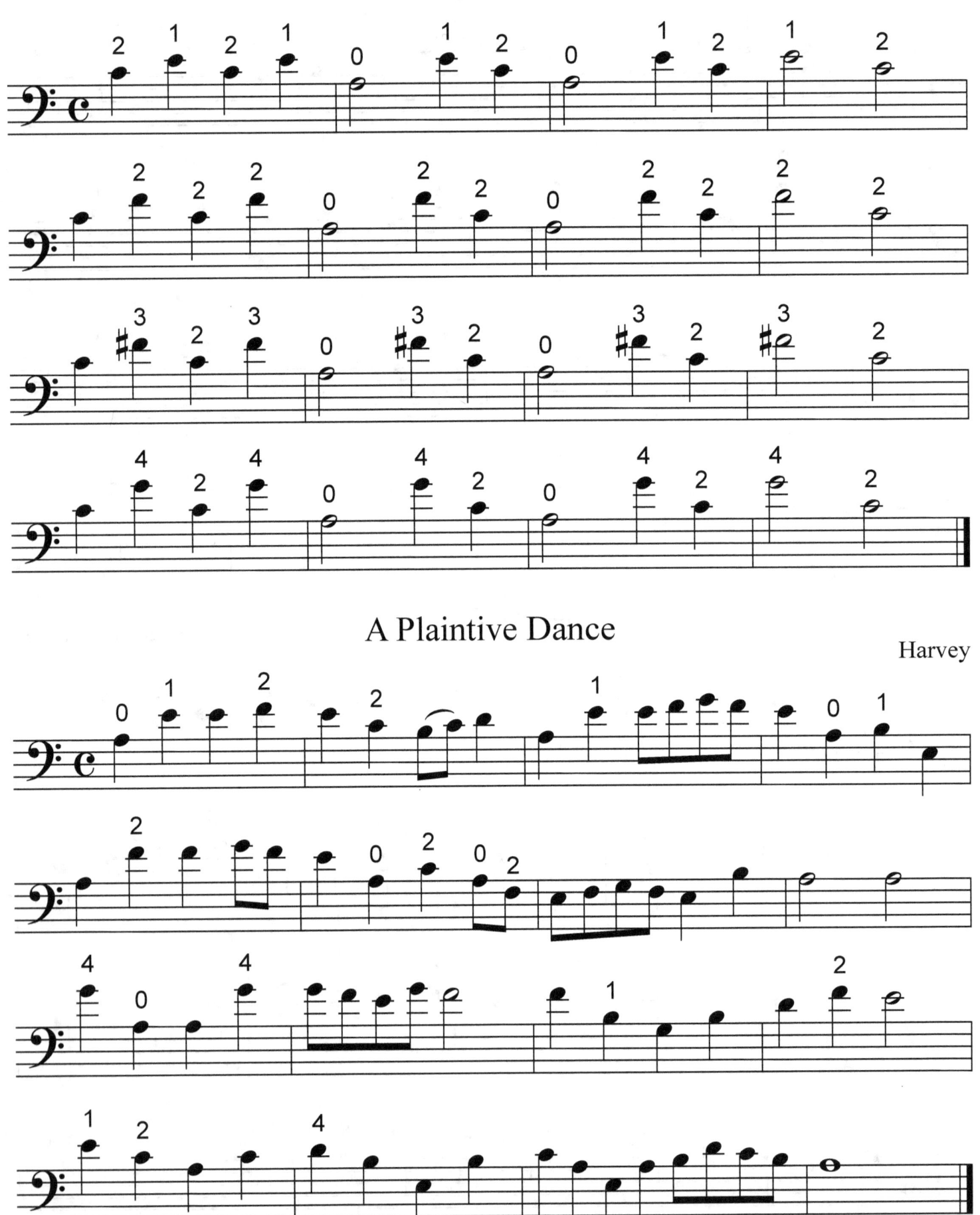

36. Shifting Back from Fourth Position

Mon Vieux Wagon

Trad., arr. Harvey

Fourth Position Preparatory Studies for Cello

37. The Hare's Trot

Trad., arr. Harvey

38. Alpenklänge

Wohlfahrt, arr. Harvey

available from www.charveypublications.com: CHP272

Flying Fiddle Duets for Two Cellos, Book One

John Ryan's Polka

Trad., arr. Myanna Harvey

©2015 C. Harvey Publications. All Rights Reserved.

www.ingramcontent.com/pod-product-compliance
Lightning Source LLC
Chambersburg PA
CBHW051426070526
44584CB00023B/3607